KILLERS OF THE ANIMAL KINGDOM

TIGERS

KATHLEEN A. KLATTE

PowerKiDS
press

New York

Published in 2020 by The Rosen Publishing Group, Inc.
29 East 21st Street, New York, NY 10010

First Edition

Editor: Elizabeth Krajnik
Book Design: Reann Nye

Photo Credits: Cover Setta Sornnoi/Shutterstock.com; p. 4 Popova Valeriya/Shutterstock.com; p. 5 dptro/Shutterstock.com; p. 6 dangdumrong/Shutterstock.com; p. 7 seng chye teo/Moment/Getty Images; pp. 8, 16 Ondrej Prosicky/Shutterstock.com; p. 9 PhotocechCZ/Shutterstock.com; p. 10 Sarawut Aiemsinsuk/Shutterstock.com; p. 11 Stanislav Duben/Shutterstock.com; p. 13 Chaithanya Krishnan/Shutterstock.com; p. 14 Sasha Samardzija/Shutterstock.com; p. 15 Picture by Tambako the Jaguar/Moment Open/Getty Images; p. 17 neelsky/Shutterstock.com; p. 18 jeep2499/Shutterstock.com; p. 19 Gannet77/E+/Getty Images; p. 21 Subhendu Sarkar/LightRocket/Getty Images; p. 22 ehtesham/Shutterstock.com.

Cataloging-in-Publication Data
Names: Klatte, Kathleen A.
Title: Tigers / Kathleen A. Klatte.
Description: New York : PowerKids Press, 2020. | Series: Killers of the animal kingdom | Includes glossary and index.
Identifiers: ISBN 9781725306219 (pbk.) | ISBN 9781725306233 (library bound) | ISBN 9781725306226 (6 pack)
Subjects: LCSH: Tiger–Juvenile literature.
Classification: LCC QL737.C23 K53 2020 | DDC 599.756–dc23

Manufactured in the United States of America
CPSIA Compliance Information: Batch #CSPK19: For Further Information contact Rosen Publishing, New York, New York at 1-800-237-9932

CONTENTS

BLACK, WHITE, AND ORANGE

Tigers are beautiful members of the cat family. Many people have seen tigers in zoos. They're easily recognized for their orange fur with white bellies and black stripes. Sometimes, a tiger's stripes are brown or gray.

Tigers live in a number of different **habitats** in Asia, from Russia to Sumatra. Tigers are solitary animals, which means they live and hunt alone. These giant predators are apex predators, which means they're at the top of the food chain and they have no natural predators. They're carnivores, which means they eat only meat. Read on to find out more about these striped hunters!

Tigers are large predators with sharp teeth, powerful **jaws**, and big claws for hunting and killing their **prey**.

5

TIGER SUBSPECIES

All tigers living in the world today belong to the same **species**, *Panthera tigris*. Scientists have grouped tigers into different subspecies depending upon where they live, their size, and their **genetic** makeup. However, scientists often disagree about how many subspecies of tiger there are.

KILLER FACTS

Bengal tigers are the largest group of tigers living in the wild— about half of all living tigers. The largest population of Bengal tigers lives in India.

Sometimes Bengal tigers have white babies. This happens when both a mother and a father tiger carry a type of gene that controls the coat color of their baby. White tigers are very rare in the wild.

Some scientists believe tigers should be separated into six subspecies. The Bengal (Indian), Siberian (Amur), Sumatran, Malayan, and Indochinese tigers can be found in the wild. The South China tiger may exist only in zoos today. Other scientists believe tigers should be separated into only two subspecies: the tigers of mainland Asia and the tigers of Sumatra, Java, and Bali.

7

TIGER HABITATS

Tigers used to live in many parts of eastern and southern Asia, as well as in some parts of central and western Asia and the Middle East. Over time, tigers' **ranges** have gotten smaller. Today, tigers are found in a number of different habitats. They like living in forests, swamps, and grasslands. However, no matter what type of habitat tigers live in, their range only goes as far as their prey is found.

Tigers that live in warm places, such as **tropical** islands and rain forests, like the water and are strong swimmers. They will swim to cool off or to chase prey.

Tigers have **adaptations** to help them live in their habitat. For example, tigers that live in colder places grow heavy fur in the winter and have large, padded feet to help them move through snow.

9

TIGER SIZE

Tigers are the largest members of the cat family. Siberian tigers are the largest subspecies of tiger. Male Siberian tigers can grow to be about 13 feet (4 m) long and weigh up to 660 pounds (300 kg). A tiger's tail may be as long as 3 feet (0.9 m). Female tigers are shorter and weigh less than males.

Tigers look different and are different sizes depending on where they live. Tiger subspecies tend to be smaller the farther south they live. Sumatran tigers are the smallest and lightest living subspecies. Males are about 8 feet (2.4 m) long and weigh about 260 pounds (117.9 kg).

BLENDING IN

Tigers hunt their prey by sneaking up on it and attacking. Even though you may think a tiger's fur would make it stick out, it actually helps it blend in. When the sun shines through the trees and leaves, it makes shadows. The tiger's stripes look a bit like these shadows.

Tiger stripes also break up the parts of the tiger's body shape, making it hard for their prey to see them. This type of camouflage, or blending in, is called disruptive coloration. When a few tigers are together, their stripes can make it hard for their prey to tell how many tigers there are.

KILLER FACTS

Each tiger's stripes are one of a kind, just like a person's fingerprints. No two tigers have the same pattern of stripes. Scientists use tiger stripes to tell which tiger is which.

Tigers' stripes also help them blend in with grasses. They wait for prey to pass by and then they attack!

13

ON THE HUNT

Tigers are most active at night. Because they're solitary animals, they usually hunt alone. They have large paws that help them balance on different surfaces. Their paws are padded to help them sneak up on their prey. Tigers have strong bones and muscles in their legs to help them run after, jump, and grab their prey.

KILLER FACTS

One of the most famous types of tigers wasn't actually a tiger. The saber-toothed tiger is an **extinct** catlike animal about the size of a modern lion or tiger. They're well known for their huge fangs.

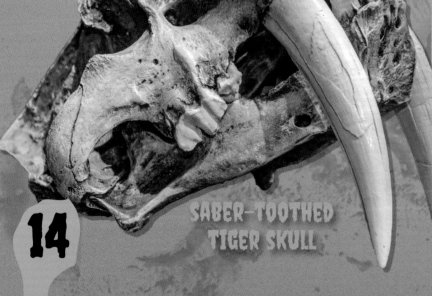

SABER-TOOTHED
TIGER SKULL

A tiger's claw can be up to 4 inches (10.2 cm) long. They scratch trees to keep their claws sharp for the next kill.

Tigers have long, curved claws that retract, or pull back, into their paws. This helps keep their claws sharp. Tigers use their claws to hunt and sometimes to climb trees. Tigers' large fangs, or sharp front teeth, are among the largest of any big cat.

15

SHARP SENSES

Tigers depend most on their senses of sight and hearing to hunt their prey. Their eyes can see when there isn't much light, which helps them hunt at night. A tiger can see about six times better than a human in the dark.

Tigers have very good hearing. In fact, it's their sharpest sense! They're able to move their ears to hear sounds that their prey makes. This lets them know where their prey is.

Tigers' eyes face forward, allowing them to see how far away something is and helping them move around their habitat to hunt their prey.

Tigers don't usually use their sense of smell for hunting. However, they may use it to tell if they're in another tiger's range or if a female is ready to have babies.

A TASTY MEAL

Tigers eat many different things, from pigs to elephant calves. Their main prey weighs about 45 pounds (20.4 kg) or more. However, they'll eat smaller animals if that's all there is to eat. Tigers eat, on average, one deer-sized animal a week.

KILLER FACTS

Tigers will hunt and eat whatever is available. If people make farms within a tiger's range, the tiger may prey upon the farmer's animals. If a person gets in the tiger's way, the tiger may kill and eat the person.

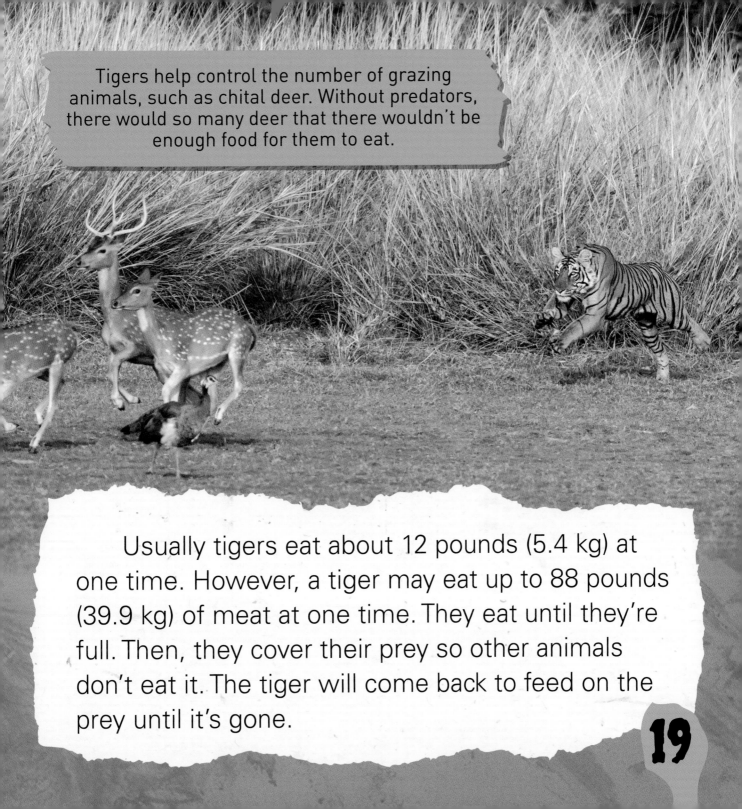

Tigers help control the number of grazing animals, such as chital deer. Without predators, there would so many deer that there wouldn't be enough food for them to eat.

Usually tigers eat about 12 pounds (5.4 kg) at one time. However, a tiger may eat up to 88 pounds (39.9 kg) of meat at one time. They eat until they're full. Then, they cover their prey so other animals don't eat it. The tiger will come back to feed on the prey until it's gone.

PEOPLE AND TIGERS

Tigers have been a part of human beliefs and art for thousands of years. In the past, people have used tiger body parts because they believed the parts acted as medicine or had healing powers. This is untrue.

Even though there are laws to protect tigers, people often hunt the tigers for their beautiful fur. In the last 100 years, tiger numbers have gone from as many as 100,000 down to as few as 3,200.

Today, people kill tigers because tigers kill farm animals and may hurt people in nearby towns. As people continue to move farther into tigers' ranges, attacks on humans happen more often.

KILLER FACTS

Three subspecies of tigers have gone extinct in the last 100 years. Today, you won't be able to find any Caspian, Javan, or Balinese tigers.

Tigers are an important part of Hindu mythology. Hinduism is a set of beliefs practiced by some people in India.

21

TIGER CONSERVATION

Fewer than 5,000 tigers are left in the wild. Many groups of people and zoos are working hard to protect these important creatures and educate people about why tigers matter. Countries have passed laws to make it illegal to kill tigers and sell things made from tiger parts. This is called conservation. Because of conservation, tiger numbers are rising.

Other groups build special areas called wildlife reserves for tigers to live without people poaching them. Zoos help raise tiger numbers by helping tigers have babies. Scientists work hard to study tigers and their habitats. All of these efforts can help tigers become plentiful again.

GLOSSARY

adaptation: A change in a living thing that helps it live better in its habitat.

extinct: No longer existing.

genetic: Referring to the parts of cells that control how a living thing looks and grows.

habitat: The natural home for plants, animals, and other living things.

jaw: Either of the two bony parts of the face where teeth grow.

prey: An animal hunted by other animals for food.

range: An area of land or water where a species of animal lives and hunts.

species: A group of plants or animals that are all the same kind.

tropical: Of, relating to, occurring in, or used in the tropics.

INDEX

WEBSITES

Due to the changing nature of Internet links, PowerKids Press has developed an online list of websites related to the subject of this book. This site is updated regularly. Please use this link to access the list: www.powerkidslinks.com/kotak/tigers